Cape Ann

A PHOTOGRAPHIC PORTRAIT

First published in the United States of America by
PilotPress Publishers, Inc.
110 Westchester Road
Newton, Massachusetts 02458
Telephone: (617) 332-0703
http://www.PilotPress.com

and

Twin Lights Publishers, Inc.
10 Hale Street
Rockport, Massachusetts 01966
Telephone: (978) 546-7398

ISBN 1-885435-07-X

10 9 8 7 6 5 4 3 2

Book design by
SYP Design & Production
http://www.sypdesign.com

Cover image: Alan Murtagh

Printed in China

Cape Ann

A PHOTOGRAPHIC PORTRAIT

PILOTPRESS PUBLISHERS · TWIN LIGHTS PUBLISHERS

ACKNOWLEDGMENT

PilotPress Publishers and Twin Lights Publishers wish to thank all of the photographers who submitted their work for our consideration. Because of space limitations, we were unable to include many excellent photographs in *Cape Ann: A Photographic Portrait.* Cape Ann is a fertile area for many talented resident professional and amateur photographers. The natural beauty and spectacular clear light of Cape Ann, attracts visitors to record its special qualities at all times of the year.

Thanks go also to Deborah Carlson, Ted Larsen, and David Piemonte for judging the Cape Ann Regional Photographic Contest. The large number of entries and the variety and excellent quality of the photographs made this a very difficult task. We are pleased with their selections and are indebted to them.

We extend our appreciation to Rockport Publishers, Inc., of 33 Commercial Street, Gloucester, MA 01930 for providing the aerial photographs.

We are grateful to Lee Kingman Natti, the writer of the captions for the photographs. A longtime resident of the Lanesville area of Cape Ann, as Lee Kingman she has written many books for children and young adults, among them *The Best Christmas, Catch The Baby!,* and *The Year of the Raccoon.* As Lee Natti, she was a member of the Folly Cove Designers, famed for their use of Cape Ann subjects in their block-printed designs. Her mission in writing the captions was to find an evocative title for each photograph and to add facts to bring out history and local color, rather than describe the picture or how it was technically achieved. We think she has succeeded and given an added dimension to the book.

Finally, our thanks go to designer Sara Day for her creation of a beautiful book that tells the story of Cape Ann. As she has lived on Cape Ann all of her life and knows it well, she has been able to arrange the photographs in meaningful groups that convey the true essence of the area.

INTRODUCTION

"It is beautiful; and here I would like to fix my dwelling."
—Thorwald the Norseman, A.D. 1004

Like Thorwald the Norseman, we have found Cape Ann to be a beautiful place in which to dwell, whether as year-rounders, summer residents, or as visitors passing by for a day or a week. Be it ocean vistas, marshes, lakes, ponds, beaches, quiet wooded lanes, secluded quarries from another time, working fleets of fishing and lobster boats, modern sailing vessels or some from our past, wild life and glorious flowers that flourish near the sea, the colorful patch work quilt of the city or the towns, and the changing palette created by nature, the uniqueness of the scenery needed to be captured for posterity.

Cape Ann: A Photographic Portrait is an attempt to capture the essential quality of this special region as it is viewed and recorded by photographers—from professionals with tripods to amateurs with instamatics—all artists who see the scene and frame it with their sensibilities.

As well as enjoying the views reproduced in this photographic portrait, we hope the book will inspire your own explorations of the area, to experience your own impressions, absorb the beauty and be renewed.

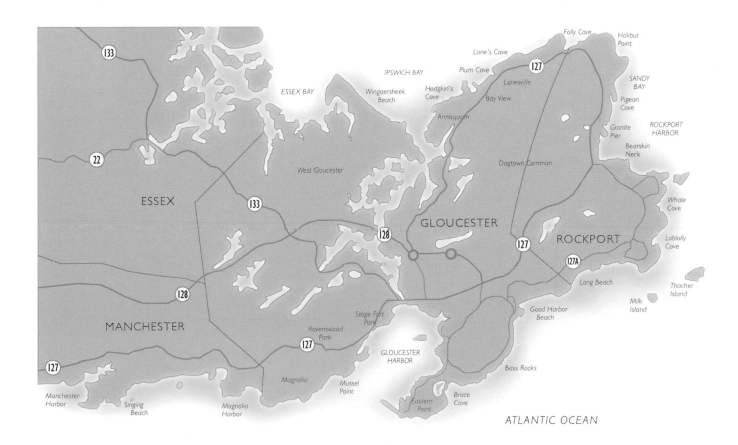

First Place

CITY HALL FROM STAGE FORT PARK

ALAN MURTAGH
NIKON 8008S, VELVIA F:11

A cold winter dawn spotlights the most prominent feature of Gloucester's skyline—the towers of City Hall. Appropriately this view is from Stage Fort Park, where the first men to dwell on Cape Ann came ashore.

Second Place

FINE DINING

NICHOLE WADSWORTH
MINOLTA MAXXUM, KODAK
GOLD 400 ASA

*The waters beyond Thacher's
Island provide seafood
entreés for a hungry hump-
back and a gaggle of gulls.
Whale watching and bird
watching are important
recreational activities in
the Cape Ann area.*

Third Place

HARBOR HOMES
PAUL MURPHY
CANON F-1, F:11,
EKTACHROME

Above the wharves, boats, and main streets of Gloucester, sturdy houses quilt a hill. From the early 1700s, when houses and businesses related to fishing and foreign trade were built beside it, the waterfront has been the city's focal point.

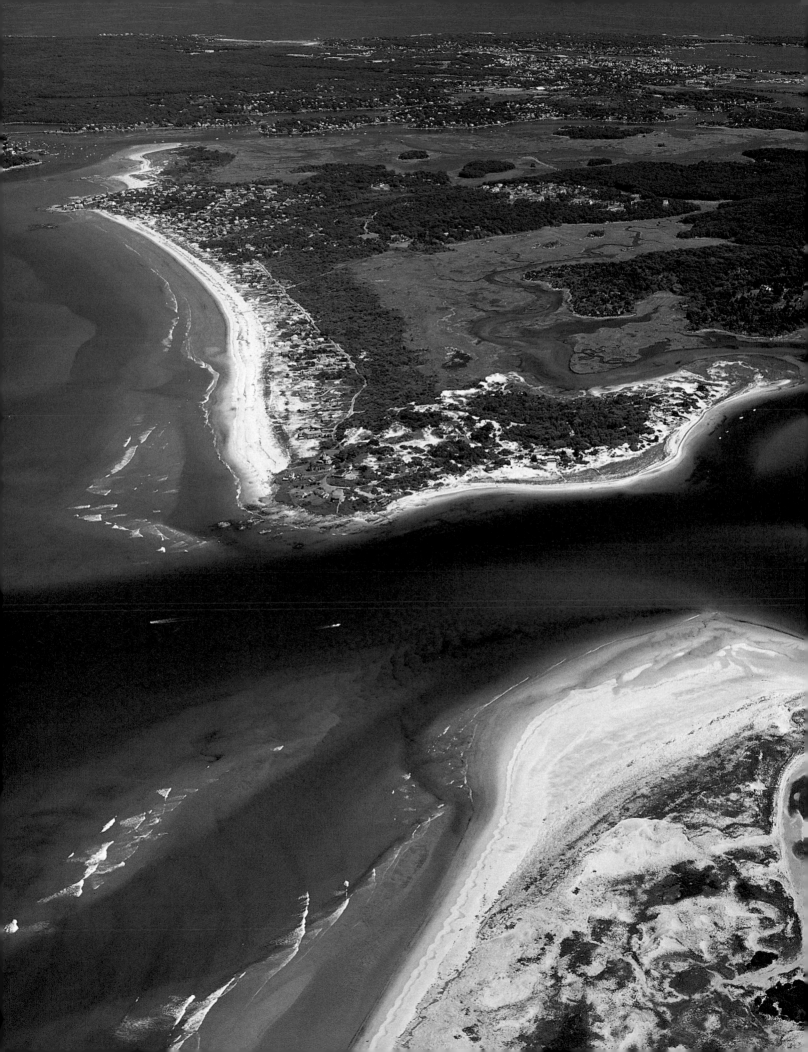

ESSEX

2

1

RESTORATION

DANIEL SAUNDERS
MINOLTA, KODAK 400 ASA

The Evelina Goulart was built in 1927 as a swordfishing boat and later connverted to use as a dragger. Rescued in a badly deteriorated condition, the Evelina may never take to the water again, but the Essex Shipbuilding Museum is raising money to restore her as an exhibit on ship construction.

2

MIRROR ON THE MARSH

THOMAS UNDERWOOD
CANON AE-I, F: 8 1/60,
KODAK SELECT 100

High tide brings Eben's Creek close to the Mabel Burnham House which over the years has become such an Essex landmark for artists that it is sometimes called Motif #2— after Rockport's famed Motif #1.

2

1

AUTUMN SIGNALS

LEN WICKENS
RICOH, FUJI 100 ASA

A colorful fall day forewarns that boats will soon be taken out of the water and stored, shrink-wrapped, in nearby boatyard. The Essex River in winter is often dotted with ice-fishing shacks.

2

TIDEWATER TRANQUILITY

LEN WICKENS
RICOH, FUJI 100 ASA

Shipbuilding began on the tidewater Essex River, then called Chebacco, in 1668 and continues to this day. The Town Landing, host in summer to small boats, is close by the site of an historic boatyard and the Essex Shipbuilding Museum.

2

1

2

3

1

FOUND OBJECTS

LEN WICKENS
RICOH, FUJI 100 ASA

The White Elephant Shop is an Essex landmark, long known as a source of objects, useful or exotic, to satisfy a need or a fancy. Essex, originally a part of Ipswich known as Chebacco, became a town in 1819 and today is known for its antique stores and seafood restaurants.

2

LOBSTERS TO GO

ERICA BETCHER
CANON AT-Z, F: 4 1/125, 100 ASA

Woodman's in Essex is famous for lobsters served in the rough, fried clams a delight they claim to have originated and the clambakes they cater to the North Shore. Clamdiggers and lobstermen, restaurateurs and cooks are respected professionals who contribute greatly to the local economy.

3

THE FINE ART OF ANTIQUING

KATHLEEN GIADONE
CANON AE-1, F: 8/250, KODAK SELECT 100

Art and antiques, collectibles, pre-owned objects, even stuff frankly labeled junque, can be found in every style of shop along several miles of Route 133 as it runs through Essex.

2

Along with a dinghy to take him down river and an anchor to secure it, a clamdigger needs rubber boots, a clam fork, buckets, a willingness to work long hours in all weathers, and a strong back. Essex is famous for its clams. Both fried and steamed, and for the restaurants that serve them.

Nor' easters batter the shore shifting creeks and sifting sand dunes. The roots of beach grass help to anchor sand and build up dunes, so replanting beach grass is important in trying to save battered beaches.

2

1

A PORCH WITH A VIEW

ALAN MURTAGH
NIKON 8008S, F:11, VELVIA

Artists are often seen at their easels in the yard of the Mabel Burmham house near Farnham's, on Route 133. The beautiful marshes that border Eben's Creek and stretch out toward Hog Island are a challenge for painters and photographers in all seasons.

2

SEQUESTERED

ALAN MURTAGH
NIKON 8008S, F: 5-6, SENSIA

Creeks wind through the Essex salt marshes providing sheltered moorings for boats and pools where herring gulls, varieties of ducks, and even great blue herons seek food.

1

RECONSTRUCTED

ALAN MURTAGH
NIKON 8008S, F: 8, SENSIA

In 1998 a Chebacco boat was once again being built in the Essex shipyard. To be named the Lewis H. Story, she will be displayed as the flagship of the Essex Shipbuilding Museum. The Chebacco, a two-masted boat with a pointed bow and stern, was designed for fishing in the choppy waters off Cape Ann and used in the 1700s.

2

WAITING FOR WIND

ALAN MURTAGH
NIKON 8008S, F: 8, SENSIA

Mists, fog, and calm weather are part of any shore summer. The river and the many coves of the Essex coastline shelter pleasure craft and working boats just waiting for the right moment to venture forth.

I

1

AFLOAT

ALAN MURTAGH
NIKON ELZ, F: 11, SENSIA

*Long before roads tied shore
dwellers and growing coastal
communities together, wooden
boats, both small and large,
moved people and goods. The
tradition of keeping a boat
handy for work or pleasure
still exists.*

2

**FULL MOON, WILD
FLOWERS**

ALAN MURTAGH
NIKON 8008S, F:11, SENSIA

*Over a road that winds down
to the sea a full moon rises
in the evening sky and wild-
flowers frame a field. Many
picturesque roads thread
through the quiet fields
of Essex.*

2

GLOUCESTER

2

BOAT PUZZLE

BRENDA AHLSTROM

*The shapes of boats and their
reflections are fascinating
subjects for painters and
photographers. Artists who
give summer painting classes
frequently bring students to
Lane's Cove for the view and
the inspiration.*

2

LOW TIDE AT THE COVE

BRENDA AHLSTROM

*Whatever type it is—a row-
boat, a pram, a skiff, or a
dinghy—a small flat-bottomed
boat is essential, if only to get
from the pier to a bigger boat
moored farther out. Ladders,
too, are needed at Lane's
Cove as there is an 8-foot
difference in water level
between high and low tides.*

2

1

SAFE HARBOR

BRENDA AHLSTROM

In the 1820s granite quarries on northern Cape Ann needed loading piers and safe harbors for boats which carried stone to Boston and other ports. At Lane's Cove, a pier and a breakwater of huge granite blocks were built and today lobster boats and pleasure craft swing safely at their moorings.

2

THE WORKING HARBOR

DIANE L. BURKE
PENTAX K1000, KODAK 150, 200, F:11

Docks and boats fit together as tightly as puzzle pieces, as the daily business of fishing and lobstering takes place. Some whale-watching boats dock on the waterfront and there is a town landing where smaller visiting craft tie up and passengers come ashore.

2

1

GEAR TO GO

SUSAN HAMMER
MINOLTA MAXXIMUM AF,
KODAK MAX 400 ASA

*The hard work on a fishing
boat doesn't end at the dock.
Between trips gear needs to
be checked, nets may need
mending, and order restored
out of chaos. Before modern
filaments were developed, nets
were dried on huge wooden
reels and rewoven with a bob-
bin of twine.*

2

BUOYS DRYING

BRENDA AHLSTROM

*A lobster pot rests unseen on
the bottom of the sea so the
lobsterman uses a rope to
haul up each pot and a buoy
to float on the surface and
mark each pot location. Each
lobsterman paints his buoys in
a distinctive color or pattern
so he can find his own pots.*

I

1

ATLANTIC MARINER

JOHN D. WILLIAMS
NIKON 6006 SLR. TAMERON
2880 KODAK GOLD 200

Scavenging gulls are waterfront optimists as boats go about unloading a catch. Atlantic Mariner is a dragger that will fish far offshore for days at a time. Her wheelhouse carries electronic gear for locating fish.

2

HOME WITH THE CATCH

JOHN D. WILLIAMS
NIKON 6006 SLR, KODACOLOR
200 1/250

The inner harbor is a busy commercial area where larger vessels can dock at the State Fish Pier. Several big companies buy, process, store in freezers, and ship out fish and fish products. Smaller boats can tie up at wharves which rim the inner harbor.

3

DOCKED

JOHN D. WILLIAMS
NIKON 6006 SLR, TAMERON 2880
KODAK GOLD 200 1/250, F:16

Although government regulations now limit the catch of overfished species, the harbor is still home to working vessels. The Fishermen's Wives of Gloucester is one group that has worked hard to develop recipes to promote the use of less known species, such as monkfish, skate, and catfish.

2

3

3

1

PARKING DIAGONALLY ONLY

VAIL CART TYLER
OLYMPUS OM2, FUJICHROME 50

The North Shore Arts Association in East Gloucester is on Reed's Wharf by the harbor. During the summer it provides two floors of gallery space for paintings and sculpture by its members who include national- ly-known as well as fine local artists. Parking is adequate for all comers in all seasons.

2

BEACH COMPOSITION

JOSHUA ROSENBERG
NIKON 6006, W/SIGMA 2470MM LENS, KODAK GOLD 200

The barnacled rocks, iridescent blue mussels, and the tough- bladed grass all help to hold the beach in place.

3

PATTERNS

JOSHUA ROSENBERG
NIKON 6006, TAMRON 75-300M, KODAK GOLD 200, 1/120 @ F:8

A kildeer, an infrequent beach-goer, occasionally likes to forage for food in tide pools. Even a winter walk on Good Harbor Beach will provide interesting patterns in the sand.

1

2

3

1
PRACTICE DOESN'T MAKE PERFECT

LINDA BRAYTON
MINOLTA AF, TELEPHOTO

A popular event for brave participants and cheering spectators is the greasy pole, part of Gloucester's St. Peter's Fiesta held each June. Walking the greased pole is tricky and dumps most contestants into the water. Few victors succeed in reaching the flag at the end of the pole.

2
FIESTA FLOAT

WILLIAM J. FERREIRA
PENTAX SPOTOMATIC,
KODACHROME 64, F:11/125

Each June the Italian community honors St. Peter with a fiesta. A procession of colorful floats, some representing religious figures, parades the statue of St. Peter to a facade by the water front where a solemn mass is celebrated on Sunday morning.

3
A FAMOUS FLEET

SHARON LOWE
CANON T70, FUJICOLOR SUPER HQ 100

Seine boats are built to hold several rowers and still have room to carry big seine nets. The nets are thrown from the boat to catch surface fish like mackerel and herring.

THEY THAT GO
DOWN TO THE SEA
IN SHIPS
1623 ◆ 1923

3

1

BAY WATCHER

LEN WICKENS
RICOH, FUJI 100 ASA

Overlooking Ipswich Bay the Annisquam Lighthouse stands on Wigwam Point, so named because Indians once summered there. First built in 1800–1, rebuilt in 1897, the lamp was lit by sperm oil and then kerosene until it was electrified in 1922. In clear weather the lamp's flash is visible for 15 miles.

2

THE MAN AT THE WHEEL

ROBERT A. DENNIS
NIKON N70, KODAK GOLD

Leonard Craske's bronze statue of a Gloucester fisherman standing steadfast to his course at sea was erected to mark the 300th anniversary of Gloucester. It stands symbolically on a block of Cape Ann granite on Stacy Boulevard overlooking the harbor in honor of those lost at sea.

3

WAITING FOR A BITE

ROBERT A. DENNIS
NIKON N70, KODAK GOLD

The Dog Bar Breakwater, constructed of Cape Ann granite and completed in 1905, makes Gloucester Harbor a more sheltered haven, It is 1100 feet long with a lighted beacon poised at the end. Its huge blocks provide a good walk for the agile and a fine place for an angler to try his luck.

1

1

HEADING OUT

ALAN MURTAGH
NIKON 8008S, FUJI SENSIA, F:5-6

Heading toward the open sea past Dog Bar Breakwater on a calm day is no problem for a boat captained by a local fisherman. Large vessels of foreign registry which bring fish to the processing and freezer plants along the waterfront require the help of an experienced harbor pilot.

2

EVENTIDE

LEN WICKENS
RICOH, FUJI 100 ASA

Looking out to sea beyond Gloucester Harbor stands the famous statue known as The Man at the Wheel. It is an evocative symbol of the courage and fortitude of the fishermen who have made the name Gloucester known all over the world.

3

TOWER AND TURRETS

ALAN MURTAGH
NIKON EL2, FUJICHROME 100, F:11

A unique view from Stage Fort Park catches the dominating clock tower and turrets of Gloucester City Hall. Erected in 1870–71, it contains a large auditorium which has hosted plays and concerts, sporting events, graduations, city-council meetings and a national sculpture show.

2

3

3

1

MASTS AND SPIRES

WILLIAM J. FERREIRA
PENTAX SPOTOMATIC,
KODACHROME 64

The tower of City Hall is a distinctive Gloucester land-mark at any time of day. On the Cape, those who want dra-matic scenes can watch the sun rise out of the Atlantic in the morning and set over the waters and shore line of Ipswich Bay.

2

DAWN WELCOME

MICHAEL HUBLEY. NIKON F5,
35105
@ 105, FUJI VELVIA, F:22 1/8

Sunrise services are often held on Easter morning at Good Harbor Beach, and at any time and tide of the year the dawn there may be spectacular.

3

AFTERGLOW

JOSEPH P. CAPOBIANCO
NIKON FG TELESOR 75-300M,
F:5.6 @ F:5.6 100M. +0.5 ON
TRIPOD

When visitors to the rocks by the Annisquam Lighthouse leave and the afterglow fades, the Light will once again become a steady sentinel.

1

2

3

1

COOL WATERS, WARM SANDS

LEN WICKENS
RICOH, FUJI 100 ASA

Beyond Good Harbor beach, Salt Island is close by and further off is Thacher's Island, on which stand the landmark Twin Lights. Thacher's is named for Anthony Thacher who with his wife was washed ashore from a boat wrecked in the hurricane of 1635.

2

SPRING

CINDY SCHIMANSKI
KODAK, SHINON

Gardens brighten Cape Ann from crocus time until chrysanthemums have finally faded. Route 127 around the Cape is particularly lovely when roses are in bloom.

3

GOOD HARBOR BEACH WITH ROSES

LEN WICKENS
RICOH, FUJI 100 ASA

Windsurfers now enjoy the challenge of the bay once known by fishermen as No Good Harbor. The beach, bordered by dunes and beach roses, has fine sand, occasionally warm water, and a wonderful expanse at low tide for toddlers and builders of sandcastles.

3

1
GLOUCESTER SKYLINE

LEN WICKENS
RICOH, FUJI 100 ASA

Between the blue-topped towers of Our Lady of Good Voyage Church is the figure of Mary carrying a fishing boat in her arms. Built in 1915 by a large Portuguese community, the church honors the Portuguese fishermen and fleet. One tower contains a carillon, the first in this country, on which summer concerts are played.

2
STONE AND BRONZE

ARLENE TALIADOROS
NIKON N-90, KODACHROME, F:11

Designed in 1850 by artist Fitz Hugh Lane, a seven-gabled house of granite overlooks Gloucester Harbor. The rugged house makes a striking contrast to a bronze statue of the frail artist at work. A collection of his paintings are at the museum of the Cape Ann Historical Association in Gloucester.

3
VIGILANCE

ROBERT A. DENNIS
NIKON N70, KODAK GOLD

In the days of sailing vessels, rounding Eastern Point was often hazardous. The U.S. Government authorized the building of a lighthouse and keeper's cottage and Eastern Point Light first flashed its signal on New Year's Day, 1832. For many years the U.S. Coast Guard has maintained the property.

3

2

3

1

AFLOAT AND AGROUND

SALLY SMITHWICK
NIKON, ZOOM LENS, FUJI
200 ASA

*Every fishing boat has a name
and a long story, even one
that has come to a sad end.
Swans, of course, now belong
in the harbor as much as they
belong in fairy tales.*

2

**HONORING FITZ HUGH
LANE**

STACY RANDELL
DISCOVERY 270 200M. KODAK
35 MM 200 ASA

*This bronze statue honoring
reknowned American artist
Fitz Hugh Lane (1804–1865),
was sculpted by Al Duca of
Cape Ann. Gloucester is fortu-
nate to have many Fitz Huge
Lane paintings on display at
the Cape Ann Historical
Association.*

3

CONTEMPLATION

SALLY SMITHWICK
NIKON, ZOOM LENS, FUJI
200 ASA

*The harbor seal is no stranger
to the Cape Ann shore and
can make itself comfortable
on rocks and docks while it
contemplates the scene—or
snoozes. Fishermen and lobstermen are not always
pleased to see them as
they can be a nuisance.*

3

Patiently Waiting

CAROL A. SAMPSON
CANON EOS REBEL II, FUJI
200, ASA

Lanesville is sometimes
referred to as part of North
Gloucester and many of its
residents enjoy living on quiet
lanes even if it means a walk
to the main road to pick up
the mail.

Within Sound of the Sea

WILLIAM J. FERREIRA
PENTAX SPOTOMATIC,
KODACHROME 64, F:11/125

Tucked into the woods on a
Lanesville road near the ocean
is a house brightened by flowers. The sound of waves wash-
ing against the rocky shore not
far away is sometimes just an
insistent murmur but it can
turn into a roar.

Ten Pound Island Light

SHARON LOWE
CANON T70, FUJICOLOR SUPER
HQ 100

The lighthouse on Ten Pound
Island was first lit in 1821
and a house was also built
for the lighthouse keepers.
Winslow Homer boarded there
in the summer of 1880 and
painted some fifty watercolors
of scenes around the harbor.

1

1

HAMMOND CASTLE

LEN WICKENS
RICOH, FUJI 100 ASA

John Hays Hammond, Jr. built his castle with large spaces for his laboratory, his art collection, his home, and a grand 10,000-pipe organ on which famous organists have performed. Inside, he mixed romanesque, medieval, and renaissance architecture, and, outside, a statue of himself looking out to sea.

2

A CASTLE BY THE SEA

CHRISTOPHER WALTER
MINOLTA XG7, 200 ASA.

Now a museum, Hammond Castle was built in the 1920s by John Hays Hammond, Jr., a brilliant inventor. Before World War I Gloucester residents were startled to see a passengerless boat moving about the harbor as Hammond ran it by remote control from his laboratory.

2

1
AT SAWYER POND

LEN WICKENS
RICOH, FUJI 100 ASA

On Cape Ann, to find a covered
bridge (this one on private
property) is unique. Sawyer Pond
could be named for Samuel
Sawyer, a leading Gloucester
citizen who bequeathed to the
city the 600 acres now known
as Ravenswood Park. The public
park offers well-marked trails
and many varieties of wild
flowers and trees.

2
APPROACHES TO
GLOUCESTER

LEN WICKENS
RICOH, FUJI 100 ASA

In 1643 settlers cut a canal
connecting the Annisquam River
to Gloucester Harbor, and over
the years what was known as
"the cut bridge" was the only
entrance by road to Gloucester
and Rockport. In 1953, the A.
Piatt Andrew Bridge brought
Route 128 over the river,
which is still a busy waterway.

3

1

BY DAWN'S EARLY LIGHT

SALLY SMITHWICK. NIKON,
ZOOM LENS, FUJI 200 ASA

*Storms bring spectacular surf
to the rocky back shore of
Gloucester and on calmer days
it is still worth a lingering look
at the unbroken expanse of
ocean at any time of day, The
almost two-mile stretch along
Atlantic Road, known as Bass
Rocks, is a favorite place for
joggers, walkers, artists and
photographers.*

2

PARADE REST

PAUL MURPHY
CANON F1, EKTACHROME, F:56

*Two tall-masted schooners at
anchor give only a tantalizing
glimpse of how the harbor
must have looked when the
fishing fleet consisted of
sailing vessels.*

3

SUNSET SAIL

KIMBERLY HOWLETT
CANON AE-1, KODAK, PRINT
FILM 100, 125/5.6

*A sunset glow reinforces the
red paint which makes the
Paint Factory a prominent
landmark on Rocky Neck. The
Tarr & Wonson Company won
international awards for their
copper paint which was used
on the bottom of wooden
boats to deter barnacles and
other marine growths.*

1	2	3
TRANSFORMATION	**LOOKING IN**	**SYNCHRONIZED ROWING**
CAROLE AMORE MINOLTA, 400 SI MAXXIMUM, 200 ASA, F:4	WILLIAM J. FERREIRA PENTAX SPOTOMATIC, KODACHROME 64, F :II/125	SALLY SMITHWICK. NIKON, ZOOM LENS, FUJI 200 ASA

Many dusty and noisy quarries were operated on Cape Ann from the 1820s to the 1920s. The use of granite for paving and building dwindled and the industry died. Steep-sided deep quarries slowly filled with water and many have been transformed to peaceful places with houses built around them.

Magnolia lies between Gloucester and Manchester-by-the-Sea and at one time was an elite summer resort of grand towered and porched hotels. Its arcaded Lexington Avenue was lined with exclusive shops. Many summer homes are now used year-round.

Dories were used for two men, or dory mates, to row off from their schooner and set out their long lines of hooks— scenes brought to life in the movie Captains Courageous. In recent years dory races are an exciting summer event with intense rivalry between Cape Ann and Nova Scotian teams.

3

3

After The Rain

GRENVILLE ROGERS

Ten Pound Island, rumored to have been bought from an Indian for ten pounds, probably was named by mackerel fishermen who could stake ten ''pound'' nets, or weirs; around it, or even for the pounds, or pens, put there for sheep (by town vote: "rams onlie").

Double Vision

ANN STICKNEY
MINOLTA SRT 201, FUJI 100

A double promise of calm after the storm is reassuring to the beach-goers and to residents of a house which has survived many ferocious storms, among them the infamous No Name Storm of 1991.

Mother and Child

JULIE H. RICARD
CANON T 20 TELEPHOTO,
KODAK 800 ASA @ 1/125

A mother and calf stay close together as they surface off Stellwagen Bank. Whale Watch boats leave Gloucester several times a day in summer and within an hour reach prime areas for spotting humpbacks and minkes, and occasionally a rare right whale.

3

1

BOWSPRIT—THE SPIRIT OF MASSACHUSETTS

MARK GEORGIAN
VIVITAR V 2000, KODAK ROYAL
GOLD 150, 100, F:16

The Spirit of Massachusetts, a gaff topsail schooner, was built in 1984 as a symbol of the proud days of sailing ships. Owned by The School for Children in Arlington, MA, she is used year-round in programs for young people and as a training ship.

2

INSPIRED

ALAN MURTAGH
NIKON 8008S. FUJI VELVIA, F:11

The first Universalist Congregation was formed in 1779 in Gloucester by John Murray and the church, built in 1806, was described in a Boston newspaper as "elegant. . . and capacious" with a "beautiful spire". A landmark for ships returning to port, the spire is a prominent feature of the city's skyline.

3

ON PARADE

MARK GEORGIAN
VIVITAR V 2000, KODAK
ROYAL GOLD

Tall ships visited the harbor in August 1998 for Port Celebration Week, a part of Gloucester's 375th Anniversary. Whether seen from on board a vessel or from the shore, the ships were an inspiring sight.

3

1

SETTING THE SAIL

JOHN D. WILLIAMS
NIKON N70 SLR TAMERON
75-300. KODAK GOLD 200
1/250, F:16

*Gloucester has been host to
tall ships several times in
recent years and a parade of
sail in the harbor is a magnifi-
cant sight. These students on
the HMS Bounty, perched aloft
amid the complicated rigging,
are unfurling one of the sails.*

2

SIGHTS TO SEE

LEN WICKENS
RICOH, FUJI 100 ASA

*Schooner Day in Gloucester
has become an annual event
at the end of summer. Just
as a schooner under sail is
dramatic and facinating, so is
the Hammond Castle, now a
museum, located on the
Magnolia shore.*

3

UNDER SAIL

MARK GEORGIAN
VIVITAR 2000, KODAK GOLD
100, F:16

*The original H.M.S. Bounty
was a British war vessel, a
frigate designed for speed. The
replica, which visited
Gloucester in 1998, was built
for use in the movie Mutiny
on the Bounty and is owned
by a private corporation.*

MANCHESTER-
BY-THE-SEA

3

SHORE VISION

LEN WICKENS
RICOH, FUJI 100 ASA

The Arbella arrived in 1630, to be greeted by forerunners who called their hamlet Jeffrey's Creek. On board Arbella the men of the Dorchester Company brought with them a charter which would establish the Massachusetts Bay Colony and give it a measure of independence not formerly granted to a colony in the new world.

HISTORIC HOUSE

ROBERT DENNIS
NIKON N70, KODAK GOLD

The Federal style Trask House is now a museum and home for the Manchester Historical Society. Richard Tink, whose far-sailing square-riggers made him a successful merchant, changed his name to Trask at the request of his wife, Abigail, who wanted a more substantial-sounding name. She kept a store in the house and sold dry goods, bonnets, and rum.

HURRAY FOR THE FOURTH

KIMBERLY HOWLETT
CANON AE-1, KODAK GOLD 100, F:8 @ 250

Manchester's July 4th parade passes by the Town Hall decorated with a monumental flag. Small-town parades are personal; costumed children on floats hail their picture-snapping parents and friends greet neighbors driving siren-screaming fire engines. Balloons escape, backyard barbecues sizzle, and on occasion fireworks light up the harbor.

1

SHELTERED HARBOR, SHELTERED HOMES

LEN WICKENS
RICOH, FUJI 100 ASA

An ocean view, whether from a boat upon the water or a house overlooking it, is a privilege. Views, space, and privacy make up an important part of Manchester-by-the-Sea's ambience and reputation.

2

SINGING BEACH

ROBERT DENNIS
NIKON N70, KODAK GOLD.

The warm sands of Singing Beach are a comfort to bathers who have tested the usually cold Atlantic waters. The beach has been a favorite view for photographers and painters, among them Winslow Homer whose Eaglehead, Manchester, MA shows the sweep of the beach toward the point of land so named.

2

1

HARBOR VISION

LEN WICKENS
RICOH, FUJI 100 ASA

When Arbella dropped anchor
in "a fyne and sweet harbor" in
1630, Masconomo, Sagamore
of the Agawam Indians, paddled
out to greet her. Among the
passengers were the poet Anne
Bradstreet, her husband Simon,
and her father Thomas Dudley,
both future governors of
Massachusetts Bay Colony. Ever
since the local inhabitants have
greeted sailors and celebrities
with aplomb.

2

REFLECTION

LEN WICKENS
RICOH, FUJI 100 ASA

Turtle Pond on Route 127 is a
place where one may ponder a
true reflection of a peaceful
scene. A few years ago some
lively scenes were filmed here
for the movie Mermaids, which
starred Cher.

3

ECLECTIC

DANIEL SAUNDERS
MINOLTA 100 ASA

A weathered shack gains character from the collection of
lobster buoys, the American
flag, and the potted plants
that adorn it, while the rain
barrel, the chopping block, and
the woodpile tell of the
shack's usefulness—shelter.

2

3

2

HARBOR WELCOME

LEN WICKENS
RICOH, FUJI 100 ASA

The Rotunda, as it is called,
on Tuck's Point is a pleasant
place from which to observe
sailors in their boats on a
sunny day, or, in the moonlight,
to propose marriage. In summer the harbor is crowded
with yachts and sailboats. The
Manchester Yacht Club celebrated its 100th anniversary
in 1992.

AUTUMN BLAZE

LEN WICKENS
RICOH, FUJI 100 ASA

Manchester-by-the-Sea is
also known for tranquil
places which offer quiet
escapes from fast-paced
living. in earlier days large
estates served as summer
retreats for the wealthy, but
as the town is within 45 min-
utes by car or train from
Boston, it is now year-round
home to many commuters.

2

1

WINTER AT SINGING BEACH

MICHAEL HUBLEY
NIKON N90S, FUJI VELVIA, 75-
300 @300, F:8 @ 4. 81A FILTER

Although storms have pounded
Singing Beach for centuries, so
far the character of the sand
remains the same: hard needle-
like crystals of quartz and zircon
that rub against grains of softer
feldspar. This causes a sound
described as a sneaker squeak-
ing on a gymnasium floor.

2

SERENITY

JAY OKER
NIKON 35MM, KODAK 64 @ 2 1/4
ROLLI KODAK 64

The solemn standing stones
mark the difficult lives and
too-early deaths of the early
settlers. 1661 is the date
memorialized on the wrought-
iron gate, although the first
date to be found on a tomb-
stone is 1714.

2

I

REFRESHMENT

A. HENRY JONES
MINOLTA SRT 101, 800 ASA

*On the shore gulls can always
find tidbits and momentary
rest. In early days boats enter-
ing the shallow inner harbor
had to watch the tides or be
stranded on mud flats as the
tide went out, but by 1896
dredging made the inner
harbor navigable for larger
vessels.*

2

A NEW DAY

MICHAEL HUBLEY
NIKON F5 24MM, F:22 @ 1/2

*A sweep of changing tides
and a rosy dawn bring a
peaceful moment to a beach
that will later hum with sun-
worshippers, castle-builders,
and brave bathers.*

1

ENLIGHTENMENT

A. HENRY JONES
MINOLTA SRT 101, 800 ASA

Places of worship and learning are emphatic in the life of a town. The First Parish Church, Congregational (1809) is an example of late Federal architecture. The cockerel weathervane (1754) atop its spire is dented by arrows shot by a Penobscot Indian. The stone-walled Public Library (1887) was designed by Charles McKim.

2

SUNSTAR

MICHAEL HUBLEY
NIKON 90S 75-300 @ 300, F:16 @ 1, 81A FILTER

The solidity of Eagle Rock at Singing Beach seems shattered by a ray of sun, as waves below crest and batter at the shore.

3

CALM AT COOLIDGE POINT

SHARON LOWE
CANON T70, FUJI SUPER HQ 100

The financier Thomas Jefferson Coolidge was a benefactor who provided the town with its public library. In 1902 he built his stately summer residence, known as The Marble Palace, on a commanding point of land. Three generations of men named Thomas Jefferson Coolidge have hosted presidents and princes there.

2

3

R O C K P O R T

2

I

PREPARATIONS

JOHN D. WILLIAMS
NIKON N70, TAMERON 75-300
KODAK GOLD F:5-6 @ 1/250

*A fisherman sculls his dinghy
with a long pole as he goes
out to board his boat, taking
along his bait and his gas can.
Clad in a heavy sweatshirt and
waterproof overalls, he is pre-
pared for colder and rougher
weather beyond the harbor.*

2

ROCKPORT ICON

DONALD SEIFFERT
NIKON FA W/N IKON 50-135MM
KODAK GOLD F:3-5

*Rockport's fame was spread in
1933 when locals created a
27-foot-long model of Motif #1
to enter in the parade of floats
at the American Legion
Convention in Chicago. Accurate
in every detail, from the rigging
on the fishing boats alongside
its dock to the shack's chim-
ney, the model won first prize.*

1

2

3

1

ONE OF A KIND

STEVEN BALLARD

Torn loose from their pots by storms or cut loose by boat propellors, stranded buoys are beach collectibles. Each one in this collection is different— painted with the pot-owner's distinctive colors and designs.

2

HARBOR RIGHTS

JOHN D. WILLIAMS
NIKON N70, SLR TAMERON 28-80,
KODACOLOR 200, F:11 @ 1/250

In the 1990s, the fishermen and lobstermen of Pigeon Cove banded together to fight local and state authorities over their loss of some rights in the cove. They won the long battle and talented local friends produced and performed in a grand musical about the battle.

3

GEAR TO GO

GRENVILLE ROGERS
MINOLTA KODAK 800 ASA

Pigeon Cove on the north of Cape Ann is a small harbor where tidy shacks lining the quay are protected by a high stone breakwater. In its store at the end of the quay, the Pigeon Cove Fishermen's Cooperative sells the freshest of fish, and also lobsters, which are shipped by air all over the country.

3

1

HANNAH'S HOME

LEWIS SOFMAN
NIKON F-4 4, FUJI REALA 100 F:22

Hannah Jumper (1781–1865) was a spinster, seamstress, and herbal healer who, at age 75, was horrified by the town's rampant alcoholism. She organized and led 200 women armed with hatchets and hammers who in one day in 1865 smashed every keg and bottle in every bar and tavern in town. Rockport has voted itself dry ever since.

2

SANTA, HO!

EILEEN FORD
OLYMPUS OMG W/200 M
ZOOM LENS

Santa Claus takes time each year to pay a visit to Rockport and arrives in port by boat. In Dock Square he greets children and admires the beautifully lighted Christmas tree there. Rockport also celebrates with a traditional outdoor Nativity pageant which attracts hundreds of awed onlookers.

3

NEAT HARBOR, TIDY TOWN

MABEL COONEY
MINOLTA, PRINT FILM 400 ASA

Above the trim boats and tidy buildings stands the steeple of the Old Sloop Congregational Church which in 1814, during a period of privateering and piracy, was hit by a cannon ball fired from a British frigate. The skirmish is referred to as The Battle of Sandy Bay.

1

2

GUARDIANS AND THE SEA

SHARON LOWE
CANON T70, FUJICOLOR
SUPER HQ 100

*From Long Beach the Twin
Lights stand out, marking the
length of Thacher's, a small
island on which the U.S. Coast
Guard, the U.S. Fish & Wildlife
Department, and the Town of
Rockport all have interests.*

HARBOR MOORINGS

STEVEN BALLARD

*Sandy Bay lies off northern
Cape Ann from Pigeon Cove to
Straitsmouth, with Rockport
Harbor providing the most
shelter. The popularity of sailing, yachting, and regattas in
the 1880s led to the organiz-
ing of a Sandy Bay Yacht Club
in 1885 and its clubhouse,
floats, and moorings were
established in the 1930s.*

2

2

1

Due Warning

STEVEN BALLARD

In 1771 two lighthouses were built on Thacher's Island, and were replaced in 1861 with the well-known Twin Lights. Today the southern light which flashes a red beam is maintained by the Coast Guard. The northern light is owned by the Town of Rockport Thacher's Island Committee, which strives against odds of time, tide, and money to keep a yellow light aglow.

2

Winter Hazards

PETER PRYBOT
NIKON N70, KODAK GOLD
MAX 400, F:5-6

Even within the shelter of Pigeon Cove, a boat can take a fierce battering by wind and tide, so boat owners stop by often to check their lines and moorings. Sturdy wire lobster traps now almost entirely replace the picturesque but more easily broken wooden traps of earlier days.

3

Tea Time

CAROL A. SAMPSON
CANON EOS REBEL II, FUJI
200 ASA

*"No grumps" are allowed at
Rozie's Tea Time & Kab
Kompany, although trolls are.
Gardeners on Bearskin Neck
grow astonishing amounts of
greenery and flowers from
window boxes, pots, and
tiny plots.*

2
Flower Show

JOAN M. PROTO
CANON 2135, KODAK MAX

*Bearskin Neck offers a profu-
sion of flowers, salty breezes,
sparkling water views, and
good food including chowder,
lobster, strudel and pastries.
Distinctive galleries and shops
feature everything from
authentic ship models, fine
jewelry, clothing, toys, arts and
crafts, whimsy (at Half Moon
Harry) to a country store.*

3
Garden with a View

VIRGINIA M. GRANDISON
CANON PRIMA 35MM, KODAK
GOLD 200, F:5.6

*Whether it is the salty air, the
occasional misting of fog that
affects the plants, or just the
pure light that artists cherish
on Cape Ann, flowers by the
sea seem to have a special
brilliance and depth of color.*

1

2

3

1	2	3
PERSPECTIVE	**SUMMER PURSUITS**	**PORT OF ENTRY**
CAROL A. SAMPSON	PAUL MURPHY	LEWIS SOFMAN
CANON EOS REBEL 11, FUJI	CANON F-1 AGFACHROME F:11	NIKON N 5, FUJI REALA 100, F:11
200 ASA		

All over Cape Ann colorful buoys have themselves become a decorative motif.

The juxtaposition of lobstering and tourism occurs on a town landing by the harbor as visitors enjoy the sun and the sea.

Fishermen still use shacks on Bearskin Neck to store their gear and with a bit of artistic livliness, display their own kind of decoration.

1

1

SWEET PROFUSION

VIRGINIA M. GRANDISON
CANON PRIMA 35MM, KODAK
GOLD 60MM F.5.6 200

*A tiny garden in front of a
Granite Street house blooms
from early spring through
autumn with a succession of
colorful flowers of the season.*

2

OUTCROP

STEVEN BALLARD

*Gardening most anywhere on
Cape Ann is a matter of avoid-
ing underlying ledges and
obtrusive rocks—or of making
use of them, tucking flowers
into soil-filled pockets as this
imaginative gardener on
Bearskin Neck has done.*

2

1

2

3

REFUGE

FRAN SCALISI
CHINON DX, 35MM 200 ASA

An empty bench by a pleasant pond on an autumn day is an invitaion to rest and contemplate nature.

COMPOSITION

CAROL CARLSON
NIKON F1, F:22

Trees, water, and stone compose a view in Millbrook Park. The granite bridge and a granite staircase that descends from King Street are dedicated to the quarrymen and stoneworkers of Cape Ann.

MEADOW MAGIC

CAROL A. SAMPSON
CANON EOS REBEL I I, FUJI 200 ASA

Millbrook Meadow can be a quiet retreat or a merry maelstrom when a trainful of children arrive for a summer day of stories, told by talented tellers. The meadow has also hosted May festivals with song and dance around a Maypole and several acoustic guitar concerts.

2

MOTIF #1

LEN WICKENS
RICOH, FUJI 100 ASA

In the 1900s many fishing shacks were taken over by artists who painted and sometimes even lived in them. Gilbert Tucker Margeson named his shack when he realized it was the number one motif for fellow artists. In 1945 the town acquired the building as a memorial to its men and women in the armed services and Rockport artists chose the shade of red to paint it.

SWAN POND

JULIE RICARD
KONICA FC1, KODAK 400 ASA @ 1/60

A swan may seem removed from reality, a bird of majesty and mystery—part of a tale told in a book or a ballet like Swan Lake. Or a swan may be very real, floating on Henry's Pond near Pebble Beach.

3

3

1

A Likely Spot

PAUL MURPHY
CANON F-1, KODACHROME F:16

Whether the inclination is to enjoy the beach or do the town, Front Beach provides a view, some sand, cool ocean, and little eating places conveniently close together. Within quick walking distance are motels, guest houses, restaurants, galleries and shops.

2

A Motive for Reflection

ARLENE TALIADOROS
NIKON N90, KODACHROME, F:11

No wonder that the artist's eye is drawn to a harbor scene in which sky, water, boats, buildings, light and reflections compose a powerful picture.

3

Regatta Rest

LISA PATEY
OLYMPUS OM-1

Temporarily resting on Long Beach, these popular Hobie Cats await their sailors' return from a regatta lunch break. The colorful sails and the skill of the sailors make their regattas a pleasure to watch.

1

2

3

1
BANDSTAND BASH

CAROL CARLSON
NIKON F1, F:4

Musicians, organized by the Rockport American Legion Band, give frequent concerts during the summer at the bandstand by Back Beach. Their Fourth of July concert, played to cheering fans, is a rousing salute to the holiday.

2
OUT, OUT, DAMNED HOUSE

CINDY SCHIMANSKI
CHINON, KODAK

The pyre of timber that is carefully constructed each year for the bonfire at Back Beach is mischievously topped with an outhouse, and always draws cheers from a crowd grateful for indoor plumbing.

3
BLAZING GLORY

CINDY SCHIMANSKI
CHINON, KODAK

Fourth of July in Rockport features a Fireman's Parade with bands, costumed marchers, floats, fire engines exercising their sirens, and recently a marvelous brigade that performs precision manoeuvres with folding beach chairs. The grand finale is a glorious bonfire—a blazing tower of flame at Back Beach.

2

2

ANCIENT CEDARS

DOROTHY H. GAMPEL

*Telling of much earlier times—
possibly 5000 years ago if an
attempt at carbon dating is
correct—the remains of cedar
trees occasionally appear in
the sand on Long Beach when
a storm uncovers them, only to
disappear as another storm
once more buries them.*

GRANITE GRACE

GRENVILLE ROGERS
MINOLTA, KODAK 800 ASA

*The Keystone Bridge, a grace-
ful arch of granite, was constructed in 1872 with only the
keystone wedged into place to
hold it up. Under it ran the
gravity-powered Rockport
Granite Company railroad which
took stone-laden cars to piers
on the shore. Horses pulled
the cars back to the quarry.
Route 127 runs across it.*

2

1

SEA SMOKE

MABEL COONEY
MINOLTA, PRINT FILM 400 ASA

One has to love the sea and photography to be out on the beach early on a freezing February morning to capture the elusive effect of smoke rising off the water.

2

ABOARD APPLEDORE

CAROL A. SAMPSON
PENTAX K 1000, FUJI 200 ASA

With Captain Vaughn at the wheel, passengers aboard Appledore can relax as the trim yacht sails from the harbor. Any sail on a breezy sunny day along Cape Ann's coastline will provide interesting scenes, bird lore, sport fishing tales, and a sense of well-being.

3

1
WINTER RESPITE

LEN WICKENS
RICOH, FUJI 100 ASA

*Bearskin Neck, crowded with
tourists in summer and blessed
with solitude in winter, has a
history. Versions vary, but whether
it was one bear stranded on
the neck by a high tide or
several bears driven there
and killed by frightened inhabitants, the sight of at least
one bearskin drying on the
rocks gave the neck its name.*

2
WREATHS OF WELCOME

LEN WICKENS
RICOH, FUJI 100 ASA

*The Pigeon Cove Chapel on
Granite Street still gathers in
active church-goers today. Built
in 1868, with a tower and bell
added in 1873, the church has
been home to several denomi-
nations, including that of
Swedish Congregationalists.
For some years it sponsored
a hospitality program for
international students.*

3
A MOTIF FOR ALL SEASONS

LEN WICKENS
RICOH, FUJI 100 ASA

*After the Christmas shopping
season Rockport resumes its
other life—a quiet seaside
town where the harbor and its
fishing and lobster boats regain
their dominance. By May, when
the annual Motif #1 Day wel-
comes the tourist season, the
emphasis swings back to
shops, galleries, restaurants,
and throngs of visitors.*

1

2

3

1, 2

SUNNING ON THE SALVAGES

SANDY PALMER
CANON A-1, KODACOLOR
GOLD 200 ASA

Seals take over the cluster of rocks off Rockport Harbor known as the Salvages. These are the rocks that intrigued the poet T.S. Eliot when he visited Rockport and inspired his poem, Dry Salvages.

3

A DAY AT THE BEACH

LAURA BARRETT
GEGGIS NIKON 2020, KODAK
100 ASA F:16

A seal pup looks bewildered but healthy and can probably fend for himself. New England Aquarium sends out personnel to rescue sick or stranded seals and advises people not to approach seals, as they have a nasty bite.

1, 2

DOLPHIN DANCE

CAPTAIN BILL LEE

*Innovative photographer
Captain Bill Lee captures
images of frolicing dolphins
with his homemade underwater camera attached to the
hull of his fishing and salvage
boat, The Ocean Reporter.*

1

SEAFOOD SPECIAL

CAPTAIN BILL LEE

*Whether it is boiled or
steamed, drenched with
butter or pristinely plain,
devoured at a beach clam-
bake, a backyard cookout,
or a restaurant, the taste of
lobster is a unique treat.*

2

TRAPPED

CAPTAIN BILL LEE

*An underwater camera pho-
tographs a curious lobster
as it crawls toward its fate.*

CONTRIBUTORS

Brenda Ahlstrom
One Hoot Owl Way
Rockport, MA 01966

Carol Amore
105 Corning Street
Beverly, MA 01915

Steven Ballard
2313 Jenkintown
Glenside, PA 19038

Erica Betcher
48 Old Cart Road
So, Hamilton, MA 01982

Linda Brayton
527 Washington Street
Gloucester, MA 01930

Diane L. Burke
12 River Road
Merrimac, MA 01860

Raphael Bustin
288 Magnolia Avenue
Gloucester, MA 01930

Joseph P. Capobianco
4 Beatrice Road
Beverly, MA 01915

Carol H. Carlson
43 Broadway
Rockport, MA 01966

Vail Cart Tyler
2 Noah's Hill Way
Essex, MA 01929

Mabel Cooney
12 Atlantic Avenue
Rockport, MA 01966

Robert A. Dennis
18 Orchard Crossing
Andover, MA 01810

William Ferreira
77 South Avenue
Melrose, MA 02126

Eileen Ford
25 1/2 King Street
Rockport, MA 01966

Dorothy H. Gampel
6 1/2 Summer Street
Rockport, MA 01966

Laura Barrett Geggis
38 Haven Avenue
Rockport, MA 01966

Mark Georgian
57 Pearl Street
Amesbury, MA 01913

Kathleen Giadone
9 Jackson Avenue
Peabody, MA 01960

Virginia Grandison
1449 Waggamon Circle
McLean, VA 22101

Susan Hammer
73 Cottage Road
Newbury, MA 01951

Kimberly Howlett
26 Beach Street
Gloucester, MA 01930

Michael Hubley
7 River Drive, Apt. C
Danvers, MA 01923

A. Henry Jones
79 Summer Street
Manchester, MA 01944

Captain Bill Lee
4 Sunset Lane
Rockport, MA 01966

Sharon Lowe
4 Raymond Street, Apt 7
Gloucester, MA 01930

Paul Murphy
18 Wells Street
Gloucester, MA 01930

Alan Murtagh
Stock Stills Photography
P.O. Box 549
Essex, MA 01929
(978) 283-8706
e-mail: murthog@gis.net